LEEDS AT WA

JAMES M. HAGERTY

Head of Sixth Form, Corpus Christi High School, Leeds

Published by EP Publishing Limited 1981

Published by **EP Publishing Ltd., Bradford Road, East Ardsley, Wakefield, West Yorkshire WF3 2JN**

ISBN 0 7158 0767 6

First edition 1981

Printed in England by
E. J. Arnold & Son Limited, Leeds

Introduction

This collection of illustrations and documents is an attempt to record the life of the people of Leeds during the two world wars. It is not complete by any means. In a limited selection from the available evidence one can only portray glimpses of a city adapting to the conditions and circumstances of wartime. Essentially, though not exclusively, it relates to civilian life. To exemplify the varied military exploits of Leeds men and women I have, of necessity, chosen a representative sample. Those who wish to pursue the military history of the city during the First World War will find W. S. Scott's **Leeds In The Great War** of interest. There is not, as far as I am aware, a similar volume for the Second World War.

Immediately after the declaration of war in August 1914, the people of Leeds rushed to do two things – enlist and buy food. The city became like a military garrison and troops and recruits were marching everywhere, being inspected and heading for training camps. Simultaneously, those who were sensitive to the long-term nature of the crisis stocked up with provisions. Sugar, butter, ham, eggs, bread and flour rapidly increased in price. The **Yorkshire Post** reported that 'a big section of the public has lost its head completely . . .'. In music halls the portrait of the Kaiser was received with derision. Leeds folk, like many others up and down the country, felt confident that victory would be theirs by Christmas. Those who forecast a long struggle, however, were proved correct and the inhabitants of Leeds faced four years of wartime economy and military service.

It becomes more difficult for succeeding generations to understand the essence of the First World War. The moral fervour aroused by the invasion of Belgium, the enthusiasm and bravery of city battalions, the long lists of dead and wounded, the soldiers' cynicism about the civilian's total inability to comprehend the slaughter, and the controversy over war memorials were aspects of the conflict experienced in Leeds as in other communities. It has been estimated that on the first day of the Battle of the Somme (1 July 1916) every street in Leeds lost one man as the Leeds 'Pals' charged into the German machine guns west of the village of Serre; 17 out of 900 'Pals' answered the roll-call. On that day the British Army lost 15 men dead and 30 wounded every minute for 24 hours. And at home the industrial production necessary to maintain the efforts of the nation's fighting men continued as the war dragged on. Those who worked in the city's clothing industry, engineering works, munitions works and in volunteer services did so often despite personal grief and, as the explosions at Barnbow testify, hazardous conditions of employment.

The Second World War was different for both civilians and those in the armed forces. The outbreak of Hitler's war was not greeted with euphoria. People had been prepared for it. Air raid shelters, gas masks, evacuation schemes and rationing were part of a lengthy countdown to what the **Daily Herald** termed 'zero hour'. Civilians were nearer to the war than they had been during 1914–18. Leeds was bombed and civilians were killed and wounded. Non-combatant involvement was far greater and so too was the industrial output of the city. The statistics contained in this book bear witness to the vast resources of this great northern manufacturing and commercial centre.

The military experience of those from Leeds was also vastly different from that of the First World War. Gone, for example, were the city battalions. Tanks, aeroplanes, submarines and other technological advances, many of which were made in Leeds, added a new dimension to warfare although some had been used on a limited scale in the Great War. Leeds men and women served in a variety of units in many locations. To trace their contribution as a whole has been difficult. The compactness of the military history of the First World War contrasts sharply with the total war of 1939–45.

Of necessity a great deal has been omitted. Sporting and leisure activities are obvious examples. So too are details of the heroes of the Second World War – the winners of the VC and other awards for gallantry. Leeds had its share. Leeds Grammar School alone lost 83 former students and had 36 decorated for bravery or mentioned in despatches. In other cases material is hard to find – for instance, evidence relating to military hospitals in the area during the Second World War. Of the material which has been included, the anti-Jewish riots, the Leeds Convention (both of 1917), and the contribution of industry in both wars are deserving of further study.

The experience of Leeds at war is unique to the people of Leeds who live to remember it. Hopefully, after reading this book many **loiners** will feel the urge to dig out old photographs, ration books, demob papers, medals and letters and write down or tape-record their memories of themselves and their city at war.

The evidence has been collected from a variety of sources and I am very grateful to those who have located material, loaned personal mementoes and supplied information. Full acknowledgement is made at the end of the book to all those who have helped in any way. Finally, I am indebted to Frances Royle for her enthusiasm and assistance, and special thanks go to my wife Trina.

James M. Hagerty
Leeds, 1981

1914~18

The Recruiting Office in City Square. The people of Leeds like those in other cities returned from their annual summer holidays to find that the European crisis had deteriorated beyond recall. War came with little surprise. As the men of Leeds joined up, 60 Germans in the city were arrested, detained at the Town Hall and later interned.

On 6 August 1914, the **Yorkshire Post** reported: 'There were again enthusiastic scenes at the Empire and Hippodrome Music Halls in Leeds yesterday . . . the portrait of the Emperor of Austria was received in dead silence, but the portrait of the Kaiser aroused hooting from various parts of the house'.

THE LEEDS "PALS" 2nd BATTALION RECRUITING CAR. Seb 1914

Following Lord Kitchener's call for volunteers, Colonel Walter Stead, a Leeds solicitor, proposed the formation of a city battalion. As in other cities men rushed to join up and the illuminated tramcar became a feature of the recruiting campaign. 'T' Army' wanted 'British Bulldogs' and 'Airedale and Yorkshire Terriers'. 'John Willie' joined with his pals and boarded the tram for Berlin. By the end of September over 5000 men had joined Kitchener's army and in addition over 1000 had joined the Leeds 'Pals' battalion.

Although the Leeds 'Pals' became the most famous of the city battalions there were others. The Leeds Rifles (7th and 8th Battalions West Yorkshire Regiment) were formed before the 'Pals' and were soon ready for duty. Here they parade at Carlton Hill Barracks. The **Yorkshire Post** reported that 'Leeds . . . had the appearance of a town in military occupation'. Men of the Yorkshire Hussars had even brought their own horses. Smaller men were initially denied the privilege of serving King and country but later they were enlisted in the Leeds 'Bantams' (17th Battalion West Yorkshire Regiment) and sailed for France in January 1916.

An advance party of the Leeds 'Pals' unloading supplies at Colsterdale near Masham in September 1914. They had no uniforms and took with them blankets donated by the public. Aldermen Charles Wilson and Arthur Willey took on the responsibility of feeding, clothing and equipping the 'Pals'.

Members of 'B' Company, Leeds 'Pals', receive mail at Colsterdale in September 1914. They also got pipes from Ben Wade, the Leeds pipemaker, and 1 oz of Tetley's 'Golden Pelican' tobacco. There are still no uniforms but the tents had given way to huts. The 'Pals' became the 15th Battalion, West Yorkshire Regiment.

In his memoir **A Leeds 'Pal' Looks Back**, Mr A. V. Pearson of Horsforth recalled life at Colsterdale when the 'Pals' were training. Drill, sentry duty and marches were interspersed with soccer, trench digging, weapon training and leave – in Leeds. Mr Pearson was in 'C' Company and here they can be seen resting after trench digging.

The 'Pals' left Colsterdale for Fovant on Salisbury Plain and then sailed to Egypt from Liverpool on the **Empress of Britain**. Bandmaster J. Garside, Company Sergeant Major H. Gill and other members of the Battalion concert party look happy enough *en route* to the Middle East. Their joy was shortlived, however, as the transport carrying beer from Leeds was sunk.

Lieutenant-Colonel S.C. Taylor and other officers of the Leeds 'Pals' recruiting in Leeds during June 1915. The tram, with the band on the top deck, is now adorned with posters calling for 'still more' men. Over 800 recruits passed through the tram, no doubt motivated by the emotive poster 'Remember Scarborough' recalling German bombing of the Yorkshire resort.

Performances at the Empire and Hippodrome Theatres were interrupted by recruiting appeals as were soccer matches at Elland Road. Volunteers gathered on the pitch to be inspected and applauded.

Photo by Gale & Polden.

Lieut.-Col. S. C. Taylor and Officers who proceeded with the Battalion on Active Service. [3]

Back Row—Lieut. J. G. Vause, 2nd-Lieut. T. A. R. R. E. Willey, Lieut. G. S. Ward, Lieut. R. H. Rayner, 2nd-Lieut. R. H. Tolson, Capt. R. Atkinson, Lieut. H. Smith, 2nd-Lieut. A. Liversedge.

Middle Row—2nd-Lieut. M. Booth, 2nd-Lieut. L. Foster, Lieut. R. M. Blease, 2nd-Lieut. A. N. Hutton, Lieut. J. S. Pape Smith, Lieut. S. M. Bickersteth, 2nd-Lieut. J. Everitt, Capt. J. L. Armitage, Lieut. N. Evers, Lieut. E. Lintott.

Front Row—Capt. T. C. Boardall, Revd. C. Chappell (Chaplain), Hon. Lieut. and Quartermaster R. J. Anderson, Capt. P. H. Mellor, Major L. P. Baker, Lieut.-Col. S. C. Taylor, Capt. and Adjt. E. K. De Pledge, Capt. T. Gibson, Capt. G. C. Whitaker, Capt. L. Bathurst (R.A.M.C.), Capt. S. T. Neil.

Officers of the 15th Battalion, West Yorkshire Regiment – the Leeds 'Pals'.

The Leeds Rifles being inspected by the Lord Mayor, James Bedford, in May 1915. During the early months of the war the Rifles undertook training exercises and coastal patrol duty in Yorkshire and Lincolnshire. When they reached the Western Front they saw action at Ypres and the Somme. The 7th and 8th battalions won over 400 individual battle honours.

Watched by onlookers, a contingent of the West Riding Divisional Army Service Corps marches through the city centre. Some of the men, probably new recruits, are still without uniform. The RASC provided horse and motor transport and was stationed at Doncaster. The West Riding Division eventually left for France in April 1915.

Me & my Tommy

From the **Yorkshire Post**, 7 July 1915.

'A Leeds Vicar's Impressions of the British Soldier.

A Leeds vicar who has returned home after a visit to one of the base camps in France . . . said that what most impressed those at the Front was the extraordinary cheerfulness and modesty of the British "Tommy". Dealing with the spiritual life of the camp the vicar emphasised the new spirit of devotion shown by the British Army at the Front. "Religion," he said, "is now a serious matter to our fighting soldiers. The war has had the effect of making our Army a devotional army."

. . . The vicar said that during his visit he met some of the Leeds Rifles, who appeared to be immensely surprised to find that the Germans knew who they were before they had been in the trenches many minutes. It appeared that as soon as the 8th Battalion got into the trenches some of the Germans began to call out "Now Leeds".'

Bombardier Thomas Henry Longthorn and his wife Mary Ann. They lived in Carriss Street, Hunslet. As can be seen from the badge on his arm, Mr Longthorn was a wheelwright. He worked at the Co-op's Marsh Lane depot for 50 years.

1914-15

Standing (left to right) W. Morn (*trainer*), F. Webster, D. Lewis, G. Rees, J. Chilcott, F. Mirfield, W. Ward, F. Godward, B. Ward
Mr. A. Townend (*Chairman*)

Sitting (centre): F. Harrison, F. Carter, W. A. Davies, J. D. Campbell, W. H. Davies

Kneeling: J. Harland (*Asst. Trainer*), I. Jones, J. Sanders, M. Ashcroft

The Leeds sporting scene was affected by the unusual wartime conditions and by the loss of sportsmen from every code. This photograph is of the Leeds Rugby League team taken early in the war.

**WAR OFFICE,
LONDON S.W.**

8 Sept., 1914

I wish to impress upon those employed by your Establishment the importance of the Government work upon which they are engaged. I fully appreciate the efforts which the employees are making and the quality of the work turned out. I trust that everything will be done to assist the Military Authorities by pushing on all orders as rapidly as possible. I should like all engaged by your Establishment to know that it is fully recognised that they, in carrying out the great work of supplying Munitions of War, are doing their duty for their King and Country equally with those who have joined the Army for active service in the field.

Yours very truly

(sgd.) **KITCHENER**

G R

This is to Certify that *J Mather* employed by *The Kirkstall Forge Co. Ltd.* is authorised to wear *War Service Badge* numbered *55704* so long as he is employed on work for war purposes by the employer above named

D Lloyd George

Kirkstall Forge, one of the premier engineering works in the city, produced essential military equipment. Early in the war Lord Kitchener, Secretary for War, wrote to the company emphasising the value of its work. Employees were given badges and permits (one here signed by Lloyd George, Kitchener's successor) to prevent harassment by zealous patriots. In 1916, following the introduction of conscription for men, women were employed to continue the production of axles for military vehicles. By the end of the war the company had relinquished its patents on axles for horsedrawn vehicles.

The Northern Area Army Clothing Depot was centred in Leeds and at the beginning of the war the Tramway Shed in Swinegate was requisitioned. The output of textiles, however, necessitated the taking over of the King's Mills adjacent to the tramway depot. By the end of the war the number of garments being inspected averaged 750 000 per week.

In May 1915 the Cattle Market buildings in Gelderd Road were requisitioned for use as a store for cloth. 9 million yards of cloth were stored here and later another depot, belonging to the Aire and Calder Navigation, was acquired to store 3 million garments. There were additional smaller depots like the one in Park Row where 80 000 shirts were inspected each week.

Women work alongside men sorting, recording and transporting bales of cloth from Newcastle, Staffs. The women's jobs and uniforms indicate increasing female emancipation. The Northern Area, which comprised the West Riding textile region, issued 53 million shirts, 21 million pairs of army trousers, 8 million pairs of cavalry trousers, 10 million greatcoats, 24 million puttees, 89 million pairs of socks and 30 million pairs of boots.

Men and boys of the Leeds Volunteer Battalions in a country lane near Monk Fryston. At the Whitsuntide camp of 1915 and at other training camps the volunteers, some of them in doubtful physical condition, underwent strenuous exercises in preparation for either frontline duty or defence of the homeland against invaders.

Messengers and signallers, some armed, of the Leeds
Volunteer Battalions. The Volunteers manned anti-aircraft
batteries and undertook coastal defence duties. It proved
useful experience for youths later to join the Regular Army.

Parade of the Leeds Volunteer Battalions before Lord Harewood at Soldiers' Field, Roundhay, in June 1915. There were three Leeds battalions and these were part of the West Riding Volunteer Force. Initially the administration of the Volunteers was undertaken by committees but in 1916 the Volunteer movement was taken over by the War Office. Volunteers bought their own uniforms and performed day and night patrols in the city. In addition they guarded the city's waterworks and principal railway routes.

A fleet of private cars and ambulances were manned by the RASC Motor Transport Volunteers. They carried wounded servicemen from the city's railway stations to the various military hospitals in and around the city. In addition they ferried men coming home on leave to surrounding villages and towns. Here the motor cars and their drivers can be seen taking part in the Volunteers' Review at the Soldiers' Field.

'Surrender?' – 'Never!'

Males of all ages, shapes and sizes do physical jerks at Monk Fryston during the Volunteers' Whitsuntide Camp, 1915. The headquarters of the Leeds Battalions were at Carlton Barracks, the old Eccentric Club in Albion Street and also Gibraltar Barracks in Claypit Lane.

Leeds men and women also joined the Special Constabulary and Voluntary Women's Patrols. The strength of the Specials rose to 2086, and there were 97 men in an auxiliary fire brigade. Overall there was a decrease in crime.

At the beginning of the war the Leeds Joint Parliamentary Recruiting Committee was set up to encourage Leeds men to volunteer for the forces. Voluntary workers paid over 200 000 visits obtaining promises from men to enlist. By August 1915 over 47 000 men had joined up.

There were, of course, the inevitable excuses and an appeals tribunal dealt with those seeking exemption after conscription was introduced in 1916.

In addition there were subtle ways of bringing social pressure to bear upon those who did not enlist. The Vicar of Potternewton distributed forms on which were to be recorded the names and regiments of those who had answered the call. The completed list was kept in the parish church for all to see. By the end of the war over 82 000 Leeds men had been recruited.

Parish of Potternewton.

Complete list of those whose homes are in the Parish who have joined the Forces.

T is much desired by many that a complete Roll of the men on Service, as well as those who have given their lives for their Country, should be obtained and preserved.

We propose to construct such a list and keep it in some suitable manner in St. Martin's, where all can see it. I should be glad if you will fill up the necessary details of any who have gone from your home.

Such a list will be of interest for all time, and it is hoped that it will be as complete as possible, and be kept complete, as from time to time other men go.

EDWARD B. COOK.

St. Martin's Vicarage,
May, 1916.

—:0:—

 This Paper will be called for in two or three days or may be sent to me.

[SEE OVER.

23

The first convoy of wounded soldiers arrived in Leeds on 17 September 1914, having taken part in the Battle of the Marne. A crowd of 6000 watched them being taken from City Square to Beckett's Park. The alarming casualty rate meant that accommodation for the wounded became very scarce. In 1915 the old workhouse in Beckett Street was converted into a 500-bed hospital and in September of that year it was visited by King George V.

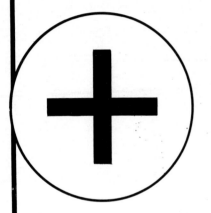

Soldiers guard the entrance to what is now St James's Hospital. During the war the old workhouse became the East Leeds Military Hospital.

ENTRANCE TO EAST LEEDS MILITARY HOSPITAL (1)

The dining hall and recreation hall at the Auxiliary Military Hospital, Temple Newsam. Lady Dorothy Wood supervised the nursing of 30 disabled soldiers from Leeds. The south wing of the house was converted into a hospital and opened on 29 October 1914, to receive, initially, Belgian soldiers. When the hospital closed on 23 November 1917, 615 patients had been cared for by Lady Wood, seven nurses and the staff of the household.

 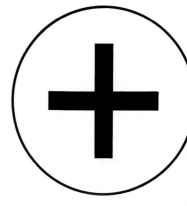

Patients and staff of the military hospital at Chapel Allerton. The hospital opened on 30 March 1916, with 35 beds. When it closed in April 1919 there were 57 beds. 1320 wounded servicemen were cared for at the hospital throughout the three years.

OBSERVATIONS
OF HOSPITAL LIFE

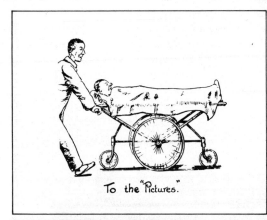

To the "Pictures."

In the operating theatre: Amusing the staff.

Chloroformed!

An impression of recollections from personal experience.

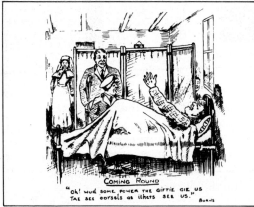

COMING ROUND

"Oh! wud some power the giftie gie us
Tae see oorsels as ithers see us." BURNS

The WIBBLY-WOBBLY WALK.

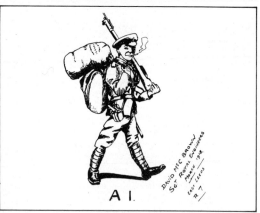

A I.

Sergeant David Brown of the Royal Engineers sketched some of his observations of life in the East Leeds War Hospital at Killingbeck. The wounded were also cared for at Beckett's Park, Gledhow Hall, and Roundhay Road School. In addition there were auxiliary hospitals affiliated to the Second Northern General Hospital in Leeds at Harrogate, Cookridge, Lotherton Hall, Stokesley, Armley, Northallerton and Thirsk.

Above: Civilians in 'boaters' and wounded men from a variety of regiments watch a parade of the Leeds Volunteer Battalions, probably in the grounds of a Leeds school.

Left: The Grand Duchess George of Russia with Privates Laycock, Roberts and Timmins at Harrogate. The three 'Pals' had been wounded in France.

Leeds never experienced aerial bombardment but elaborate precautions were taken. Special constables kept watch high in the Town Hall and were to sound the alarm on seeing the enemy. If zeppelins were sighted electricity and gas supplies were to be reduced, street lights dimmed, trams stopped, and lights subdued in cinemas, theatres and music halls. Hospitals and munitions factories were asked to reduce lights but power was not switched off. There were only two 'raids'. On 25 September 1916 and 27 November 1916, airships passed over Collingham and Pontefract Park. Incendiary bombs were dropped on Harewood House gardens but there were no casualties. The **Daily News** offered free insurance against zeppelin raids.

ACCIDENT, ZEPPELIN
AND BOMBARDMENT INSURANCE.

THE OCEAN ACCIDENT AND GUARANTEE CORPORATION, LIMITED

(Empowered by Special Act of Parliament.)

PRINCIPAL OFFICE: 36 to 44, Moorgate-street, London, E.C.

WILL PAY

ACCIDENT.

£1,000 to the legal personal representative of the bona fide holder of this Coupon Insurance Ticket if such holder shall be fatally injured by an accident within the United Kingdom to a passenger train or whilst riding in or upon any public omnibus, tramcar, or cab (which is being driven by a licensed driver) for public hire), if which such holder is at the time of such injury travelling as a ticket (or pass) bearing or fare paying passenger and will pay to such holder

£1,000

for the loss of Two or more limbs by actual separation at or above the wrist or ankle or of the sight of the eyes or of the Loss of One or more limb, as above defined, accompanied by the Loss of One or Both Eyes; OR

for the loss of One Limb as above defined or One Eye only; OR

during total disablement from earning a livelihood.

* If such holder shall so long live in "The Daily News," which are of the essence of the contract.

Provided that the above undertaking is subject to the special conditions as published in "The Daily News."

AIRCRAFT AND BOMBARDMENT.

£10,000 FREE COMPENSATION FUND.

THE PROPRIETORS OF "THE DAILY NEWS" WILL PAY

£250 in the case of damage by Aerial Attack.

£25 in the case of damage by Bombardment from the Sea, or by our own Anti-Aircraft Guns.

The Proprietors of "The Daily News" have allocated £10,000 as a FREE COMPENSATION FUND for the benefit of "The Daily News" readers, present and future, whose houses may be damaged by aerial attack or bombardment from the sea, or by our own anti-aircraft guns, subject to the CONDITIONS overleaf.

To obtain the above benefits the reader must order "The Daily News" from his newsagent and obtain from him this

FORM OF RECEIPT TO BE SIGNED BY NEWSAGENT,
AND RETAINED BY THE SUBSCRIBER.

I hereby acknowledge the receipt from

Subscriber's Signature ....

Address ....

the 2lst day of April, 1915, of an order for the delivery to his address of one copy of "The Daily News" daily from this date until further notice, and including the benefit of "The Free Compensation Fund and Accident Benefit, subject to all the conditions specified in "The Daily News" from time to time.

Newsagent's Signature ....

Newsagent's Address ....

IMPORTANT CONDITIONS: (1) To render this receipt Valid for the purposes of the Insurance, it is essential that "The Daily News" be delivered to the subscriber daily at his address, and that this receipt be signed by Subscriber prior to the Accident. (2) When claiming this receipt must be produced.

Newsagents, please note.

The house (if his own property), furniture, and household effects of every newsagent who regularly supplies "The Daily News" to customers will be covered subject to all conditions overleaf, provided he stamps and signs the form above in favour of himself.

Women employees of the Corporation Tramways Department. During the First World War 1473 women worked on the trams as conductresses. By October 1919, as men returned from the services, the number of women clippies had dropped to 64. Wages were 27s 6d for a 60 to 70 hour week in 1914. In September 1919 women were drawing 54s for a 48 hour week.

As a major industrial city Leeds became an important centre for the production of war materials. The textile industry adapted to the manufacture of uniforms whilst the engineering industry turned out components for weapons, aeroplanes, tanks and military vehicles. At the Hunslet locomotive works 4-6-0 locomotives were built for service on supply lines at the western front. Here one can be seen in action.

An outstanding fighter aircraft of the First World War was the Sopwith Camel. Pilots of this machine, which did not enter service until late 1916, accounted for 1294 enemy aircraft. 75 Camels were built in Leeds by March, Jones and Cribb in York Road. These machines served with the Royal Flying Corps, the Royal Naval Air Service and the United States Air Service. Other aircraft were built at the Olympia Works of the Blackburn Company in Roundhay Road.

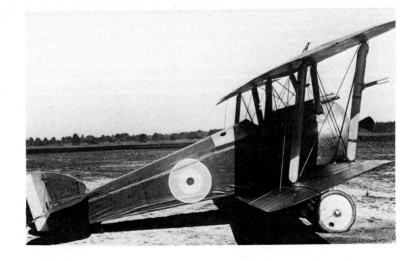

Shells being assembled at Newlay. In his **TNT Tales** T.A. Lamb wrote: 'The shell cases were first cleaned and then given a coat of khaki paint. Particulars and identification details were painted on the sides, and when dry were forwarded to the press room, trolley load after trolley load being wheeled in at the end opposite the powder entrance. Then the filling operations commenced. In order to force the powder in it was necessary to "stem" the powder – a thick stick being hammered on the top with a mallet. The crack of the mallet was almost continuous and the girls frequently accompanied the sounds by songs. Fortunately most of the songs were ragtime melodies and therefore inspired quick movement.'

Sports teams, canteen staff and fire brigade at the Royal Ordnance Factory, Newlay, Leeds. In the **Shell Magazine** O.R. Webster wrote: 'The unity of purpose and cheerfulness of spirit, with which they all work together, is strong evidence of that stern resolve and self-control, which testifies to our national temper in these historic days. Is it too much to hope that these newly awakened qualities, permeating every grade of society, will be maintained in our character during the quieter, though no less strenuous days that must follow this struggle!'

Meanwhile the **Leeds Mercury** (18 June 1917) reported other aspects of our national character:

'Raid on Leeds Gamblers.

A raid on a gang of men and youths, who were assembled on a footpath at Upper Wortley, was made on Friday night, and as a result half a dozen of them were charged at the City Police Court on Saturday with gaming at "heads and tails".'

Although food was not rationed until the later stages, food prices rose steadily during the war. The **Board of Trade Gazette** reported that between July 1914 and June 1917 fish had risen in price by 134 per cent, bacon by 80 per cent, flour by 109 per cent, bread by 100 per cent, tea by 73 per cent, sugar by 178 per cent, milk by 60 per cent, butter by 67 per cent, salt by 66 per cent, cheese by 123 per cent, eggs by 85 per cent, margarine by 68 per cent, potatoes by 114 per cent, and beef between 87 per cent and 181 per cent depending upon the cut.

The increase in the cost of all items normally entering into working class family expenditure was placed at 75 per cent.

Employees in A Shop at the Ordnance Factory, Newlay.
Wages were good but the work was dangerous and food prices were high.

1914·18

THE SHELL FROM NEWLAY

THIS is the shell from Newlay.
This is the fuse they always use in the shell that comes from Newlay.
This is the man that fits the fuse they always use in the shell that comes from Newlay.
This is the gun that is served by the man that fits the fuse they always use in the shell that comes from Newlay.

This is the gunner (not forlorn)
Who works the gun from night till morn
Along with the man that fits the fuse
They use in the shell from Newlay.

This is the quite unspeakable Hun
Who lives in dread of the 9·2 gun
That is served by the gunner (not forlorn)
Who works the gun from night till morn
Along with the man that fits the fuse
They use in the shell from Newlay.

This is the officer trim and neat
Who controls the gun from his look-out seat
And has spotted the quite unspeakable Hun
Who lives in dread of the 9·2 gun
That is served by the gunner (not forlorn)
Who works the gun from night till morn
Along with the man that fits the fuse
They use in the shell from Newlay.

This is the message sent " to fire "
That comes along a little wire
From the officer trim and neat
Who controls the gun from his look-out seat
And has spotted the quite unspeakable Hun
Who lives in dread of the 9·2 gun
That is served by the gunner (not forlorn)
Who works the gun from night till morn
Along with the man who fits the fuse
They use in the shell from Newlay.

A Blinding Flash ! A Deafening Roar !
The Huns he spotted are no more
Because of the message sent to fire
That came along that little wire
From the officer trim and neat
Who controlled the gun from his look-out seat
And had spotted the quite unspeakable Hun
Who lived in dread of the 9·2 gun
That was served by the gunner (not forlorn)
Who worked the gun from night till morn
Along with the man that fitted the fuse
They use in the shell from Newlay.

G. A. Moxon.

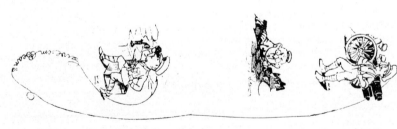

"Exeunt"

Illustrations by
W. E. KENYON.

Fire girls practise at the new Barnbow Munitions Works near Cross Gates. Note the uniform – caps, smocks and ties, puttees and boots. A fire service was an obvious necessity and the works had its own 300 000 gallon reservoir in addition to being linked to the city's water supply. Barnbow became the largest ordnance factory in Leeds employing over 16 000 people, 93 per cent being female. The factory was guarded by the Royal Defence Corps which consisted of older men.

36

Three explosions rocked the Barnbow Munitions works during the course of the war. The most serious one, in which 35 women were killed, took place on 5 December 1916, just after the night shift had started. In two later tragedies five workers, including three men, were killed. By the end of the war Barnbow had produced over 36 million cartridges, filled 24.75 million shells, fused and packed 19.25 million shells, and despatched 566 000 tons of ammunition overseas.

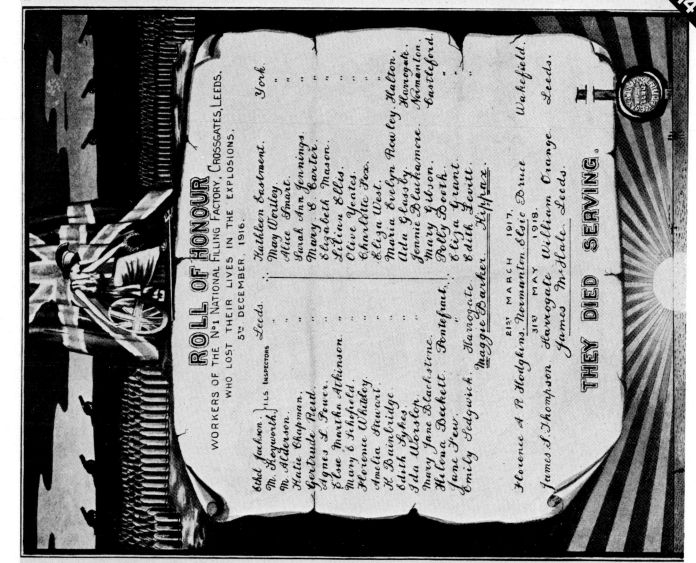

Jewish shop in Regent Street. The Jewish area of Bridge Street, North Street and Regent Street was the scene of anti-Jewish violence on 3–4 June 1917. The **Jewish Chronicle** reported that following street fights between Christian and Jewish youths there developed an ugly riot involving pit lads and older citizens. This resulted in vandalism and the looting of Jewish premises. Jewish soldiers and civilians were assaulted and the Jewish community later accused the police of complacency in the whole incident. In reporting the disturbances the **Yorkshire Post** stated that the Jews had given no cause for provocation. Of 21 000 Jews in Leeds 2500 enlisted for military service although many were exempted because of tailoring and other war work.

ARMISTICE SIGNED AT 5.0 A.M.

GERMANS TO RETIRE BEHIND THE RHINE. ALLIES' TROOPS STAND IN PRESENT POSITIONS.

Munitions workers at Barnbow, Armistice Day, 1918. Special trains carried the girls to join other workers celebrating in the city centre. 'By noon,' the **Yorkshire Post** reported, 'the city was alive with shouting, singing, merry-making crowds. As the day wore on the streets and squares became packed with people whose joy was unmistakable, and at night the unwonted illumination of shop windows ("for this night only"), and the glare of fireworks and bonfires in the suburbs (by special permission of the Chief Constable) added to the gaiety of a great day. Munitions girls were apparently the most numerous, as they were undoubtedly the most exuberant; they were everywhere. In smaller or larger groups they paraded the city carrying flags, wearing Union Jack helmets, singing "Rule Britannia", "Oh It's A Lovely War", "Good Byee", or anything . . .'

A number of charity matches were played at Headingley RFC's ground during and after the war. In April 1916, an ANZAC team played a North of England Military Team. Both sides included internationals. Some were later to die in the trenches. Of the 190 Headingley club members who joined the forces, 47 died and 22 were decorated. The Yarnbury club had 50 members in the forces of whom 14 died and four received honours; 38 members of the Leeds Grammar School club enlisted and of these seven died and two were decorated.

Six Leeds men won the Victoria Cross during the 1914–18 War. Captain George Sanders won his award at Thiepval on 1 July 1916. He was then Corporal Sanders and a member of the Leeds Rifles. Sanders, from Holbeck, also won the Military Cross in 1918. Others who won the VC were Private William Butler of Hunslet, Sergeant Albert Mountain, Private Arthur Poulter of New Wortley, Sergeant Lawrence Calvert who was born in Hunslet but lived in Doncaster, and Private Wilfrid Edwards.

Sapper Stephen Bates of Ada Crescent, Richmond Hill in the uniform of the Royal Engineers. Before 1914 Sapper Bates had worked as a flag and banner maker and then as a ladies cutter at Tainton's in Whitehall Road. During the war his wife took over his job. In May 1918 he was reported missing. He had been badly gassed and taken prisoner.

Arthur V. Pearson 15th/7ll c.coy.

A Leeds 'Pal': Arthur Pearson, who served with the 'Pals' from the outbreak of war until the Armistice. The cap badge bears the Leeds coat of arms. Mr Pearson served as a stretcher-bearer on the Somme. He later became a signaller. When demob finally came he was in Whitley Bay. There were no crowds to greet him on his return to Leeds and he was back at work within two days.

Exhibitions and displays were organised at regular intervals in order to aid the many charities established during the war. At Roundhay Park the citizens of Leeds could not only see mock air battles but also watch the testing of aeroplanes built at the Olympia Works in Roundhay Road. A large exhibition of war photographs was held during early 1919 in the City Art Gallery which had recently been the Food Control Office.

A soldier studies the 'exact reproductions' to remind himself of the horrors of war. In the days when newspaper illustrations were limited and when there were no televisions and few radios (20 amateur wireless stations were dismantled in Leeds at the start of the war) the photographic exhibition was very popular. The proceeds were either donated to war charities or to the war effort. In January 1919 Leeds raised over £4 600 000 as the city's contribution towards the cost of the war.

Children visit the war exhibition in the city art gallery. The education service in the city was affected not only by the loss of teachers and other personnel but also by the suffering and hardship experienced by pupils. Leeds children collected money for war charities and refugees, knitted socks and gloves, sent books to the troops, joined cadet corps and worked on the land.

William Malone of Devon Mount, Leeds, worked for
Tetley's Tobacco of Boar Lane, Leeds. During the Second
World War he was to serve as an ARP ambulance driver.

War memorials in the Leeds area. Below: Boy Scouts assemble outside the Stanhope Arms, Horsforth, at the unveiling of the Cenotaph in 1922. Far left is the war memorial at Farsley; in the centre is the memorial in Armley Park; and to the right is the Pudsey War Memorial. Each parish in Leeds erected some form of memorial to its fallen heroes.

1914·18

In September 1918 an exhibition of war trophies at the
City Art Gallery led to a focusing of public attention on
the idea of a permanent memorial to those who had died in
the war. After the Armistice proposals included a 'Temple of
Fame', a number of smaller memorials, hospital extensions
and even a city ring road. There was a plan to demolish
buildings in front of the Town Hall between East Parade and
Park Square to make room for the new memorial. Ultimately,
a design by H.C. Fehr was chosen and unveiled by Lord
Lascelles in City Square on 16 October 1922. The city had
lost 10 000 men.

1939~45

Military and civil defence units being inspected in the late 1930s in front of the incomplete Quarry Hill flats. Even before the Munich Crisis of 1938 there were preparations for war. By January 1939 there was a West Riding National Service Committee formed to compile a register of men and women who would eventually form the nucleus of both armed services and auxiliary civilian units.

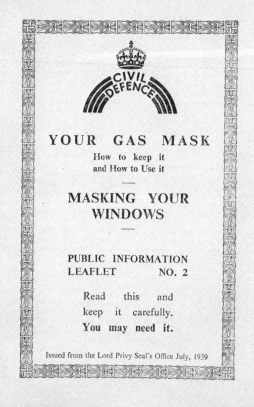

CIVIL DEFENCE

YOUR GAS MASK

How to keep it
and How to Use it

—

MASKING YOUR WINDOWS

—

PUBLIC INFORMATION
LEAFLET   NO. 2

Read   this   and
keep   it   carefully.
You may need it.

Issued from the Lord Privy Seal's Office July, 1939

---

existing shops would receive these licences. New shops would not be opened unless there was a need for them.

Shopkeepers would be instructed that they must not supply excessive quantities to any of their customers, and powers would be taken to prevent people from buying more than their reasonable share.

Maximum prices would be fixed by the Ministry for each controlled food, and would be shown clearly in the shop windows.

RATIONING SCHEME

Certain foods, soon after the outbreak of a war, would be brought under a rationing scheme similar to that which was introduced during the latter part of the Great War. In the first instance, rationing would be applied to five foodstuffs—butcher's meat, bacon and ham, sugar, butter and margarine, and cooking fats. Later, it might be necessary to add other articles.

The object of this scheme is to make certain that foodstuffs are distributed fairly and equally and that everyone is sure of his or her proper share.

Before rationing begins application forms would be sent through the post to every householder, who would be asked to give particulars of everyone living in his home. These forms, when filled in, would be returned to the local food office set up by the local Food Control Committee, which would issue the Ration Books, one for each person.

You would then register at a retail shop of your own choice for each rationed food. This registration is necessary to enable the local committee to know the quantities of rationed foods which each shop would require. There is no need to register with a shop in peace time. It is not advisable to do so.

The Ration Books would have coupons, a certain number for each week. The Ministry would decide how much food each coupon represented, and you would be entitled to buy that amount. In the case of meat, the amount would be expressed in money. Thus, you could choose between buying a larger amount of a cheaper cut, or a smaller amount of a more expensive cut. In the case of other foods, the amount would be by weight.

For children under six years of age, there would be a Child's Ration Book, but the only difference would be that a child would be allowed half the amount of butcher's meat allowed for a grown-up person. On the other hand, the allowance for a heavy worker will give him a larger quantity of meat.

For catering and other institutions, special arrangements will be made.

These are the plans for our national housekeeping in war time. Like all plans for our civil defence they need your help. In war time there would be no food to waste, but with your care and co-operation we shall have enough.

Any enquiries about food supplies in war time should be addressed:—The Director, Food (Defence Plans) Department, Great Westminster House, Horseferry Road, London, S.W.1.

51—4382 1

The government took all precautions to prepare the
civilian population for war. The above are extracts from
civil defence leaflets issued during the summer of 1939.

An Anderson air-raid shelter built in the garden of 39 Rookwood Crescent, Leeds. Over 14 000 domestic shelters were erected in the city and provided protective accommodation for 300 000 people.

When this photograph was taken in July 1939 the country had long been preparing for war. During 1938 householders received **The Protection Of Your Homes Against Air Raids**, a manual giving advice on refuge rooms, respirators, first aid, and air-raid procedure 'if there should ever be a war'.

Air-raid shelters in Leeds. Above: Surface shelters in
City Square. The picture was taken in late 1943. Note the
blackout markings on the posts. To the right is a picture
taken in 1955 of the entrance to a shelter attached to the
Co-op in Roundhay Road. Again the familiar black and
white markings can be seen.

Women preparing ration books for distribution in Leeds during November 1939. Over 4 million ration books were issued in the city during the war. For the sake of economy and the war effort almost everything was rationed and queues and shortages soon became a feature of daily life.

The health and welfare of children, however, was given priority; 70 000 tins of 'National' dried milk were given out and 12 500 bottles of cod liver oil and orange juice were issued weekly.

Boys from Roundhay School board the train for Lincoln at Beeston station on 1 September 1939.

A Roundhay boy's account of his arrival at Lincoln, taken from G. Hinchcliffe, **Roundhay School: The First Half Century**.

There were 23 boys in my party, which was guided by two young masters of Lincoln School. By now the night was coming on in earnest and in the unlighted road – unlighted because there was a practice black-out in operation – it became difficult to read numbers on gates and addresses on forms. Waiting became so long that some of us, being very sleepy, sat down on the pavement in a drooping condition. This spectacle roused the maternal instincts of the local people, who had been watching our peregrinations. Several housewives who had previously declined to take evacuees sent their husbands across the road to ask if they could change their minds. Eventually it was my turn to follow the billeting officer up the garden path. The door was opened by a lady whose face I could only dimly discern by the light of a lamp coated with blue paint. We went in, the billeting officer wrote down details on a printed form and then went out into the night, and the door was shut. I was settled in my new home at Addison Drive, Lincoln.

On 1 September 1939, 51 special trains took 18 250 children, 1450 teachers and 1350 voluntary helpers from Leeds to places of safety. The schoolchildren were taken to Retford, Lincoln, Doncaster, Worksop, Gainsborough and the Yorkshire Dales. Schools near the city centre had practised marching to the railway stations to see how long it would take when they received the call to evacuate. The children from Hunslet Nursery School found themselves transported to Bramham Park, the home of Lord and Lady Bingley.

All Communications to be Addressed to the Medical Officer of Health.

PUBLIC HEALTH DEPARTMENT,
12, MARKET BUILDINGS,
VICAR LANE,
LEEDS, 1.

J. JOHNSTONE JERVIS,
M.D., D.P.H.,
MEDICAL OFFICER OF HEALTH   ARP/29/1

Telephone 30211.

14th November, 1939.

Dear Sir or Madam,

I have pleasure in enclosing herewith
the certificate awarded to you after passing the
recent examination in Air Raid Precautions.

Will you please complete and return the
enclosed receipt form, marking your envelope
"A.R.P."

Yours faithfully,

Medical Officer of Health.

NATIONAL REGISTRATION

KGJG   5   3

Page
Micheal

Age 4 years

DO NOTHING WITH THIS PART
UNTIL YOU ARE TOLD

Full Postal Address of Above Person :—

31 Fartham St
Kirkstall Rd
Leeds 3
(Signed) Herbert Page
Date 24/5/1940

Documents of war. The registration, training and mobilisation
of the population gave rise to a tremendous bureaucracy.
Ration books, coupons, manuals, identity cards, permits –
every conceivable form of paper work reflected the total
involvement of the nation in the war effort.

No.

2 BATT/2

Local Defence Volunteers

LEEDS GROUP

8ᵗʰ WEST RIDING (LEEDS) BATTALION Company

The Bearer of this Card

MUSTILL. CLEMENT WILLIAM

NATIONAL REGISTRATION IDENTITY   K.G.A.X 184 1

C.W. Mustill.   Signature of Holder

is a Member of the Local Defence Volunteers

H.K. Doyle   Company Commander

H. J.   Group Commander

Should Service be terminated this card must be returned immediately to Company Commander

Early days of the Leeds Home Guard. Local Defence Volunteers on the rifle range. C.W. Mustill of Scott Hall Road was one of the first to join. He later commanded the 18th Battalion, West Riding Home Guard. Officers were required to attend training courses at Osterley Park run by Spanish Civil War veterans such as Tom Wintringham.

57

Two members of the Leeds City Transport Department pose behind the results of a scrap collection undertaken as part of the war effort. Railings, irons, gates, pans, and all kinds of scrap metal were collected in order to produce military equipment.

The vicar and voluntary workers preparing Southlands at Horsforth for the arrival of refugees from the Channel Islands in summer 1940. Following the fall of France and the evacuation from Dunkirk the city received hundreds of troops to be billeted with civilians.

The Headrow in wartime showing blast walls at the entrances to Lewis's and ARP water tanks in the middle of the road. Despite wartime shortages Lewis's still had all a baby needed. In addition American-style frocks sold at 47s 9d and Vel Crepe suits in battledress design were priced at 91s 6d.

Enterprising advertisements. The Co-op exploits the abnormal conditions of early wartime.

ARP ambulances in a depot of the Leeds City Transport Department. 101 private motor cars were converted into auxiliary ambulances to deal with the expected civilian casualties from air raids. In the event vehicles like these, with their headlights masked, carried only 450 civilians. The greater proportion of work was devoted to ferrying wounded servicemen to hospitals in the Leeds area.

Rescue men bring out a 'body' from the wreckage of a bombed house during a training exercise. 15 000 men and 2000 women were directed to the Home Guard or Civil Defence work. There were 132 ARP posts, 60 training centres, and over 7000 ARP wardens.

Firemen play their hoses on to the
smouldering remains of Marsh Lane
railway depot after the air raid of
1 September 1940. The fire services
in Leeds had to deal with 24 major
fires; 197 buildings were destroyed
and 7623 damaged as a result of
enemy action. There were 87 air
raid alerts. In comparison with
other areas, however, Leeds escaped
lightly. Men were sent from the city
to assist in cities like London,
Liverpool, Hull and Sheffield
where the pressure on the
NFS was much
greater.

On 2 September 1940, the **Yorkshire Post** reported that 'many bombs' had fallen on but had caused 'little damage' to a 'north-east town'. The picture it showed was this one: men inspecting a bomb crater and bomb-damaged houses in Easterly Road. Between 3000 and 4000 incendiaries and 14 high-explosive bombs had been dropped on the city.

Mr Cawthra who had experienced the raid said 'The whistling shrieks of the bombs and the thuds of the explosions punctuated the night sky and blast flashes flickered on the horizon'. The spirit of the people had not been dimmed, however, and the ARP services had risen 'superbly' to the occasion.

Drum Head Parade of the 8th Battalion, Leeds Home Guard, on Holbeck Moor, 1941. The battalion had its headquarters at Elland Road football ground. At one stage the battalion had over 5000 men. Women also joined the Home Guard. They were christened 'Army Followers' by the War Office. There were two battalions in Leeds (one north and one south of the river) and they undertook clerical and catering duties.

The Earl of Harewood accompanied by Major George Sanders, VC (wearing helmet) speaks to Sergeant William Butler, VC, during an inspection of the Home Guard at Fenton Street Barracks, 1942. The 8th Battalion must have been unique in having two VCs among its ranks. To the left of Sanders is Colonel Moncrieff.

Surface shelters and bomb-damaged houses in Model Road, Armley, after the raid of 14–15 March 1941. 77 people were killed and 327 injured as a result of nine air raids on the city. 200 damaged dwellings were cleared of furniture and other belongings, and 6556 damaged properties were repaired. Up to 66 000 people could be accommodated in the 2000 brick air-raid shelters which were built throughout the city.

1. CASUALTIES.—All serious casualties will be taken to one of the following emergency hospitals :—

Leeds General Infirmary.
St. James's Hospital, Beckett Street.
Seacroft Hospital.
Meanwood Emergency Hospital, Tongue Lane.

Minor casualties will be treated at the undermentioned First Aid Posts and any person injured should report to a First Aid Post in order that any injury allowance to which he may be entitled under the Personal Injuries (Civilians) Scheme may not be prejudiced.

Public Dispensary, North Street.
*Meanwood Road Baths.
*St. Chad's Church of England School, Otley Road.
*St. Edmund's Parochial Hall, Lidgett Park Road.
Moortown Memorial Institute.
*"E" Ward, Seacroft Hospital, Bridle Path Road.
Halton Methodist Chapel.
Harehills Lane Methodist Sunday School.
Trinity Methodist Sunday School, Roundhay Road.
*York Road Council School.
*Burley Lawn Council School.
*St. Stephen's Church of England School, Kirkstall.
*Bramley National Infants School, Town End.
*Armley Baths, Carr Crofts.
*Sweet Street (Mixed) Council School.
St. Mary's Sunday School, Baraly Road.
Middleton Child Welfare Clinic.
Waterloo Road Methodist Chapel and Sunday School.
St. Oswald's Institute, Moor Road, Hunslet.
*Dental School, Blundell Street.

* These posts have facilities for treating Gas Casualties.

2. CONTAMINATION BY GAS.—If you are splashed with liquid gas go immediately to one of the First Aid Posts mentioned in paragraph 1 which have facilities for treatment of gas casualties, or to one of the undermentioned special Cleansing Centres, whichever is the nearest.

Cookridge Street Baths.
Holbeck Baths, Holbeck Lane.
Joseph Street Baths, Hunslet.
Union Street Baths.
Bramley Baths, Broad Lane.

If you are too far away from any of these places, take a bath immediately at home or at the house of a friend or relative—speed is essential.

If you have been exposed to concentration of vapour gas only, you should remove your clothing as soon as possible and take a bath. Your clothing should be washed before it is worn again.

3. EMERGENCY FOOD AND REST CENTRES.
If you are compelled to leave your house owing to enemy action and cannot go at once to relatives or friends, go to the nearest of the undermentioned centres where food and temporary shelter will be found. If you are in immediate need of clothing it will be supplied there.

A Billeting Officer will be present at each centre and will find you a billet or other accommodation.

The Wardens or the Police will inform you of alternative centres if your nearest centre is out of action :—

Burmantofts Congregational Church, Shakespeare Street.
Congregational Church, Harehills Road.
Lady Lane Memorial Chapel, Gipton Estate.
Lakeside Cafe, Roundhay Park.
Cross Gates Methodist School, Austhorpe Road.
Templenewsam Cafe, Templenewsam.
Osmondthorpe Baptist Church, Halton Moor Avenue.
Middleton Hall, Victoria Avenue, York Road.
Richmond Hill Methodist Church.
Belgrave Chapel, Cross Belgrave Street.
Salem Chapel, Hunslet Lane.
Methodist Sunday School, Joseph Street.
St. Chad's Mission Room, New Pepper Road.
New Connexion Sunday School, Hunslet Carr.
St. John & St. Barnabas Church, Belle Isle Road.
Parochial Hall, Middleton.
Dewsbury Road Congregational Church.
Beeston Hill Methodist School, Lady Pit Street.
Beeston Hill Baptist Church, Cemetery Road.
Beeston Methodist School, Wesley Street, Beeston.
Moor Top Mission Room, New Farnley.
Bethel Congregational Church, Upper Wortley Road.
Mount Pisgah Chapel, Tong Road.
Armley Branch Road Methodist Church, Stanningley Road.
Eleven Lane Ends Methodist Church.
Moriah Chapel, Town Street, Bramley.
Kirkstall Congregational Church, Commercial Road.
Burley Perseverance Temperance Hall, Wordsworth Street.
Cavendish Road Presbyterian Church, Cavendish Road.
Woodhouse Street Methodist Church.
Methodist Church, Stocks Street, Meanwood Road.
Headingley Methodist School, Chapel Street.
Adel Methodist Church, Adel.
Shadwell Methodist School, Shadwell.
Scouts' Hut, Fir Tree Lane, Moortown.
Stainbeck Congregational Church, Stainbeck Lane.
Chapeltown Council School (Cookery Dept.), Harrogate Road.
All Hallows Church Institute, Hartwell Road.
Hawksworth Wood Methodist School, Vesper Road.
St. Edward's School, Ingram Road, Holbeck.
Alwoodley Church Hall, The View, Alwoodley.
South Parade Baptist School, Headingley.
Lidgett Park Methodist School.
Seacroft Methodist School.
Zion Methodist School, Victoria Road, Kirkstall.
Ebenezer Methodist School, Bramley.
Rodley Methodist School, Wesley Street, Rodley.
Wortley Parish Hall, Lower Wortley Road.
Cross Lane Methodist School, Farnley.
Farnley Hill Methodist School, Farnley.
Branch Road Methodist School, Lower Wortley.

Brunswick Methodist School, Bramley.
Zion Baptist School, Hough Lane, Bramley.
Bull Ring Methodist School, Lower Wortley.
Halton Congregational School, Chapel Street, Halton.
Trinity Methodist School, Tempest Road.
Parochial Hall, Meanwood.
Meanwood Methodist School, Monkbridge Road.
Leeds University Sports Pavilion, Weetwood.
St. Mary's Parochial Hall, Hawksworth Wood.
Burley Methodist School, Cardigan Lane.
St. Cross Hall, Acre Road, Middleton.
Middleton Baptist School, Middleton Park Avenue.
Middleton Y.W.C.A., Throstle Lane, Middleton.
Middleton Methodist School, Hopewell View.
Harehills Avenue Methodist School.
Trinity Presbyterian School, Harehills Avenue.
St. Cyprian's School, Colicotes Avenue.
Harehills Lane Baptist School, Harehills.
Jewish Committee's Jubilee Club, Savile Mount.
Chapel Allerton Methodist School, Town Street, Chapel Allerton.
Moor Allerton Golf Club, Nursery Lane.
St. Martin's Church Institute, Chapeltown Road.
All Saints' Parish Room, York Road.
Oak Road Congregational School, Warder Street.

4. MUTUAL ACCOMMODATION.—If you can, but have not already made mutual arrangements with relatives or friends for temporary accommodation, please do so at once.

If you have accommodation you can offer notify the Housing Dept. Annexe, 107, Portland Crescent.

5. EVACUATION TO OTHER AREAS.—If you are homeless and desire to move outside the City, you may apply at the Public Assistance Department, South Parade, for a travel voucher.

6. TEMPORARY ACCOMMODATION AND BILLETING ALLOWANCES.—A householder who voluntarily provides you with temporary accommodation will be entitled to the billeting allowances and should apply to the Housing Dept. Annexe. This will be an allowance for accommodation only. If you have no money to buy food you may apply to the Assistance Board, Cabinet Chambers, Basinghall Street, if you live in west or south-west Leeds. Residents in other parts of the City should apply to the Board's Office at 51, Clarendon Road.

7. REPAIR OF HOUSES.—If your house is damaged but can be made habitable by temporary repairs the Housing Department, 26, Great George Street, will arrange for the necessary repairs as quickly as possible.

8. CLOTHING, FURNITURE, TOOLS AND MONEY.—If you are without clothing and necessary furnishings or tools, The Assistance Board are empowered to make advances of money provided your income comes within certain specified limits.

9. SALVAGE AND STORAGE OF FURNITURE AND PROPERTY.—The primary responsibility for recovering property rests upon the owner but the Local Authority will endeavour to salvage your furniture and property, and if you are not in a position to remove and store it they will assist. Application should be made to the Housing Department, 107, Portland Crescent, for assistance or for information as to salvaged property or valuables.

If you are homeless and evacuate to another town and cannot afford the cost of transferring essential furniture to the new address you should apply to the Assistance Board Officer in the town to which you remove.

10. COMPENSATION FOR DAMAGED PROPERTY.—If a house which you own, or your own property in the house, is damaged in an air raid, apply to the District Valuer, Greek Street Chambers, Park Row, or to the Town Clerk at the Civic Hall, for Form V.O.W.1. The form must be filled in and returned to the District Valuer at Park Row within 30 days of the date of the damage.

11. INJURY ALLOWANCES AND PENSIONS FOR DEPENDANTS.—If you are injured in an air raid and are incapacitated as a result, you may make application for an allowance to the Assistance Board. This application should be made as soon as possible.

Applications for pensions for Widows, Orphans, or dependants of persons killed, or dying as the result of enemy action, should be made to the Ministry of Pensions, Regional Office, 36, York Place, Leeds.

12. EMPLOYMENT.—If you are unemployed because of enemy action you should register immediately at the Employment Exchange Eastgate. In the case of young persons under 18,

An extract from **After An Air Raid: Useful Information For The Citizen**, published during 1941 by Leeds City Council.

1939·45

City of Leeds.

The Fire Precautions (Access to Premises) (No. 2) Order, 1941.

This is to Certify *that :—*

Alfred Gaunt,

Address 9 ~~Daisy Row~~,
NEW SCARBORO ROAD
Bramley.

Is a Member of a Fire-Fighting Party organised by the Leeds City Council and possesses the powers of entry and of taking steps for extinguishing fire or for protecting property, or rescuing persons or property, from fire, which are conferred by the above-named Order.

F. Swaby.

Chief Constable.

The Town Hall in ruins after an air raid during March 1941. The City Museum was also badly damaged. Scars caused by shrapnel can still be seen on the walls outside the Art Gallery.

Winston Churchill paid a three-hour visit to Leeds during the morning of Saturday 16 May 1942. Such was the secrecy surrounding his movements that the city was given only two hours warning of his arrival. Nevertheless a crowd of 20 000 heard him speak from the Town Hall steps. His mood, the **Yorkshire Post** reported, was as 'expansive and genial as sunlight itself'. His confidence was infectious and after a speech containing the customary phrases and rallying cries he toured parts of the city in an open car with his wife. The famous 'V' sign and cigar were very much in evidence. The **Yorkshire Post** said that his visit had 'brought warmth to the streets and buoyancy to the people'.

Men of the 8th Battalion Home Guard practise firing the Smith gun at Bramley. The gun was a 3 inch smooth bore which ran on large wheels. These had to be overturned for the weapon to be in the correct firing position. At first the Home Guard was composed of static units defending railway depots, gas and electricity works, and firms such as Greenwood and Batley's. They were later absorbed into a structure based on battalions and companies thus giving both flexibility and cohesion to their efforts.

Stretcher-bearers of the Home Guard rescue a 'wounded' comrade at Bramley. The Home Guard's role became more active as the war progressed. Mobilisation was in three stages: 'stand to'; 'complete readiness'; and 'action stations'. The enemy was expected as an airborne force, an invading land force, and as sabotage squads. The Home Guard manned anti-aircraft guns at Knostrop and Adel, manned road blocks and guarded prisoners of war.

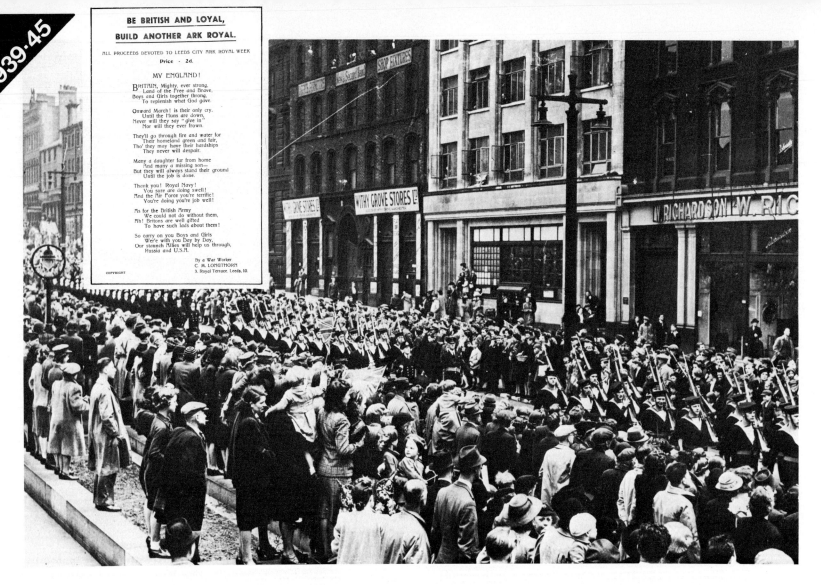

BE BRITISH AND LOYAL,
BUILD ANOTHER ARK ROYAL.

ALL PROCEEDS DEVOTED TO LEEDS CITY ARK ROYAL WEEK
Price - 2d.

MY ENGLAND!

BRITAIN, Mighty, ever strong,
    Land of the Free and Brave,
Boys and Girls together throng,
    To replenish what God gave.

Onward March! is their only cry,
    Until the Huns are down,
Never will they say "give in"
    Nor will they ever frown.

They'll go through fire and water for
    Their homeland green and fair,
Tho' they may have their hardships
    They never will despair.

Many a daughter far from home
    And many a missing son—
But they will always stand their ground
    Until the job is done.

Thank you! Royal Navy!
    You sure are doing swell!
And the Air Force you're terrific!
    You're doing you're job well!

As for the British Army
    We could not do without them,
Ah! Britons are well gifted
    To have such lads about them!

So carry on you Boys and Girls
    We're with you Day by Day,
Our staunch Allies will help us through,
    Russia and U.S.A.

By a War Worker
C. M. LONGTHORN
3, Royal Terrace, Leeds, 10.

COPYRIGHT

Citizens of Leeds watch sailors and members of the WRNS march down the Headrow during 'Ark Royal Week'. The **Ark Royal** was the city's adopted ship and over £9 million was raised. Fund-raising was apparently a success story in the city; by the end of the war over £72 million had been saved through the National Savings scheme.

Leeds schoolchildren assembled on the Town Hall steps during the 'Wings For Victory' week in July 1943. This appeal raised £7.2 million. During 'War Weapons' week over £3.5 million was raised and the fund-raising efforts during the 'Salute The Soldier' week resulted in over £6 million.

78, Ridgeway,
Roundhay, Leeds 8

Dear Barbara, I hope you are going on alright and have not had any time-bombs around your house. I told you about the stamps we were collecting at Guides, didn't I? Well, I managed to get 7,500. Boy, was Rosemary annoyed?!

We are now knitting for the Air Force, giving a concert, and either making or dressing, in patrols, a doll! We are going to have rather a busy time this winter, but still it will keep us occupied, won't it?

I am not, as you might think, writing this letter at school on the school type-writers. I have acquired a type-writerr of my own.

I hope you will excuse any mistakes that I make as I have not been learning typing very long and I am not expert yet.

Pauline Firth started work yesterday, Monday, at an Accountants at 25/- per week. Mr Firth was asking my Father how you all were, yesterday.

Mother would like to hear from your Mother just to know how she is keeping.

You ought to see my DAD in his HOME GAURD uniform. He has just got his knew ARMY uniform and it is a little too big for him, the trousers have been made for a man of 6' 2" and are a little bit tight under the arms!

We have been very lucky of late and we have had no SIRENS for weeks, touch wood, and we have been able to make up a y sleep that we lost during our busy time. Mind you we are not grumbling about it.

Grandma sends her love to everybody and I will say Goodby and Good Lck, from,
Olive

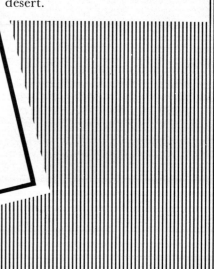

Memories of a family at war. Olive Denton typed this letter whilst still a schoolgirl. Her typing improved as she became a full-time typist on leaving school. Her husband-to-be, meanwhile, was fighting Rommel's Afrika Korps in the desert.

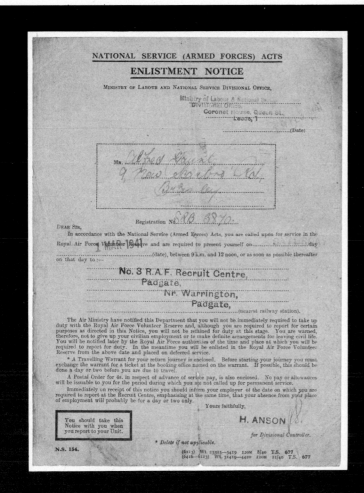

Call-up papers and a forces Christmas card. Over 100 000
Leeds men registered for military service. Unlike the
volunteers of the Great War they were not confined to local
regiments but served with a variety of units in locations all
over the world; 10 000 women enrolled for the women's services.

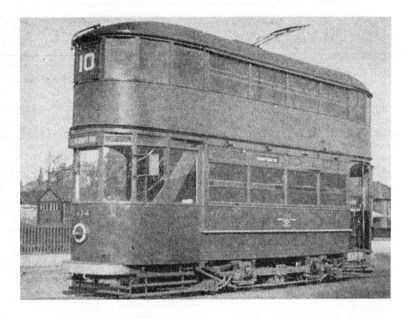

Leeds trams

DESPITE present conditions, cannot something be done to improve the Sunday evening tram service? Last Sunday I waited 25 minutes between 6 and 7 p.m. at North Hill Road stop, for a tram, getting the sixth townward one that came down.

Of the other five, four were full and the fifth had only room for two passengers.— VIATOR, Leeds 2.

Yorkshire Evening News, 19 July 1944.

Top left: One of a number of tramcars bought from Hull during the war. *Top right:* Car 474 in khaki livery and with netting to protect the windows. *Lower left:* Car 256 in Middleton woods during 1942 with blackout masks on its headlights. During the war over 1400 women were employed by the transport department.

Canteens in Leeds

ISN'T it time Leeds did something about canteens? Although there are several in the city, they prove totally inadequate to cope with the number of Service people who, through force of circumstance, are compelled to use them.

Other than the Y.M.C.A. canteen at the City Station, we have been unable to locate a canteen open after 9.30 p.m. This very overworked canteen, which is there mainly to provide refreshment for Service people who are travelling, is, at 9.30 p.m. any evening, so crowded that one has to queue for any period up to an hour to get a cup of tea and a sandwich. We know, we've queued!

We appreciate the work that is done on our behalf, but we've been stationed in smaller towns and villages where there has been at least one canteen where we could obtain something up to 10 p.m.

In Leeds, it is a choice of an evening's entertainment and no supper, or supper and no entertainment. Surely in a city of this size, something could be done about it?—SERVICEGIRLS, Leeds 8.

DOUBLE ANNOUNCEMENT!

Saturday, 11th January, 1941, at 2-45 p.m.

L.I.C.S. present their First Show

CO-OP CAPERS

COMEDY TEAM

featuring

DOROTHY RICHARDS

JACK BARKER

FRANK RUTLAND and the

8 STAR STEPPERS

New Revue for You

ORCHESTRA

J. R. Garside and F. Rutland

In

Bright, Popular Selections and Novelty Numbers

MARVELLOUS MIXTURE of MERRIMENT & MUSIC

Chairman - - Mr. J. A. SHARP (President of the Society)

Direction by JAS. R. GARSIDE

Both Shows to be held in the PEOPLES' HALL, ALBION STREET, LEEDS

Saturday, 18th January, 1941, at 2-45 p.m.

L.I.C.S. present the ever popular

ALBION FOLLIES

In an entirely new and clever show that you cannot afford to miss

LAUGHTER — MUSIC — DANCING

ARTISTES:

EVELYN SEEL (Soprano)

MADGE CHAPMAN

HILDA BROADBENT, A.L.C.M. (Pianist)

ERNEST BROWN (Baritone)

VI SCHOFIELD   MARJORIE VARNS (In their clever Song and Dance ensembles)

RENE APPLEYARD (Soubrette and Dancer)

JACK DOBSON (Ace of Comperes)

IRENE CHAPMAN

GEORGE RIDYARD (The Cheerful Fool)

The show devised and produced by GEORGE RIDYARD

Dancing Mistress: RENE APPLEYARD

THE "FOLLIES" AT THEIR VERY BEST!

LAVISH costumes

IMPRESSIVE singing

CLEVER comedy

SNAPPY dancing

Chairman:

Mr. W. M. MASON (Chairman, Education Committee)

Admission (TO EACH SHOW) **7d.** (Inc. Tax)   Members of H.M. Forces in Uniform and Children under 14 years of age **4d.** (Inc. Tax)

The Leeds Co-op did its best to keep up spirits and dividends during the war. There were regular lectures and variety performances at the Peoples' Hall in Albion Street while fellowships and clubs abounded in the suburbs. Meanwhile there were certain drawbacks to staying in Leeds as this newspaper clipping from 1944 shows.

Rescue services dealing with an incendiary bomb during a test exercise in a Leeds street. 'IBs' could start fires over a wide area and also highlight targets for bombers, but small ones could be extinguished by civilians with sand and soil.

Preliminary trimming of meat.

Immersion of a heavily contaminated sack of flour.

Loaders at work.

Special device for the treatment of tinned foods.

Fear of gas continued throughout the war. In January 1941 a food decontamination unit was set up in Leeds to deal with any emergency. There were disinfestation depots at Beckett Street and Stanley Road. The pictures here show a food decontamination exercise held in Leeds during February 1944. Liquid mustard gas had been poured over a variety of foodstuffs.

GB **6**, BB 9, Nr. 70: Kirkstallkraftwerk bei Leeds (Yorkshire).
Neues Elektrizitätswerk. Hochsp. 26,611 kV. Höchstlast 116 440 kW. Generator 147 000 kW (Gesamtleistung).

German targets in the Leeds area included the Kirkstall Power Station. This photograph is taken from the **Militärgeographische Einzelangaben über England – Objektbilder**, a book of prime targets in the north of England. An accompanying map supplied much more useful information including a list of many familiar industrial sites in the Leeds region.

THESE LOOPHOLES WERE CUT IN JULY 1940, FOR THE DEFENCE OF THESE WORKS WHEN A GERMAN INVASION OF ENGLAND SEEMED IMMINENT.

Kirkstall Forge, a major industrial installation in the city, was the target of enemy bombs on 27 and 28 August 1942. Five workers were killed in the raid which damaged the bar drawing shop and the rear axle casing shop. The Forge had its own Home Guard unit and they were prepared, as the photograph on the left shows, for the final defence of the works against German invaders.

Workers at the engineering works of Sir George Cohen and Sons, Stanningley. 14 500 women were involved in aircraft and engineering work. Here women can be seen working on the engines of Anson aircraft. Leeds and Bradford women were also employed at the Avro works at Yeadon and worked in a number of factories in Leeds producing components for Blackburn aircraft. These included the **Skua** fighter dive bomber, the **Firebrand** torpedo aircraft, the **Barracuda**, the **Swordfish**, and the **Botha**, a twin-engined medium bomber. The major firms involved were Tate's, Hudswell Clarke and Co., Appleyards, and Thomas Green and Sons.

Another achievement of the civilian war effort. In addition to a variety of other engineering products, Hudswell Clarke and Co. built locomotives. This Austerity Class locomotive was built for the War Department and is shown painted for the Leeds Thanksgiving Week Procession held in October 1945.

Women's Land Army

In 1941 there were nearly 20 000 volunteers in the Women's Land Army assisting the 540 000 male agricultural workers. By 1944, following conscription, the number of women had risen to 80 000. Caroline Longthorn (*right*) of 3 Royal Terrace, Leeds 10, was in the WLA from 1941 until 1944. With 50 other girls from the Leeds area she was stationed at Thurning Hall, East Dereham in Norfolk. The girls were led by a 'ganger' (seen on the tractor) and were contracted to local farms. Some of the girls married American servicemen from the neighbouring bases.

fashion *fashion* *fashion*

Hair Styles

FOR WOMEN AT WAR

Wartime work demands a hair style that is, above all, practical and easy to keep in order —but there's no reason why it should'nt be smart as well. If you want to know just how smart a simple hair style **can** be, ring up the Co-op Salon and arrange an appointment now with our skilled coiffeurs. They'll know exactly the style to suit you—and your job.

Perms (9 methods), full head, from 21/-

Shampoo and Set 3/-

Telephone **31333**

HAIRDRESSING AND BEAUTY SALON
A L B I O N   S T R E E T

Book your appointment NOW !

Fashions of war. 'Looking the part' as well as 'doing your bit' were apparently synonymous. The Co-op Hairdressing and Beauty Salon offered the style to suit the job. The Direct furriers promised to update old furs whilst a Leeds schoolmaster sang the praises of shorts and strapping lads.

Shorts

The suggestion recently made that secondary school boys should wear shorts until 16 has an even greater advantage now that clothes are rationed and coupons are required for purchasing them. Each pair of shorts bought instead of trousers saves three coupons. A well-made youth looks his best in shorts and stockings.

SCHOOLMASTER
Leeds.

From the **News Chronicle**, 14 July 1941.

Have Your Old Furs made Up-to-date by our **RE-STYLING SERVICE**

YOUR FUR COAT IS A WORTHY POSSESSION — even if it is old and shabby. Our experts can achieve remarkable results by reviving the skins and re-styling it to the newest fashion at small cost.

SOUND ADVICE AND ESTIMATES.

AFTER **DIRECT** *YORKSHIRE'S LEADING FURRIERS*
76 VICAR LANE, LEEDS *Tel* 29057

BEFORE

Members of the Leeds Home Guard with a Spigot Mortar, an anti-tank and anti-personnel gun which could fire bombs up to 450 yards. The various Home Guard units were responsible for the defence of localities in and around the city. The 16th Battalion and the Pay Corps with their HQ at the GPO were responsible for the central area. Other units were stationed at Kirkstall Bridge, Silver Royd, Bramley, Farnley, Low Mills, City Station and Wellington Bridge. In addition industrial sites and water supplies were guarded.

When the tide turned against Hitler and the fear of a
German invasion passed the Home Guard 'stood down'. In
rather wet conditions members of the Leeds Home Guard
took part in a final parade through the city centre on
3 December 1944.

Special Order of the Day

BY

Lieut.-Colonel C. W. MUSTILL, M.B.E.,

Commanding 18 West Riding Home Guard.

The Home Guard has stood down and the time has now come for me to send my last message to my comrades of All Ranks, with whom I have been so proud to serve.

Throughout the entire period of my command I have never called on you in vain— not once have you failed me. Your loyalty and support have made it a joy and a privilege to command you and I shall always remember you with pride and gratitude.

For four and a half years, in the face of every difficulty, you have faithfully performed your allotted tasks and you can stand down with the feeling of duty well done.

The spirit of comradeship has always been most strongly in evidence and it is my sincere hope that this spirit will be maintained through the various Old Comrades' Associations. The country will have need of all your steadiness and discipline in the difficult years which lie ahead and I ask you to carry the spirit of the Home Guard into your everyday life.

And so, for the last time, to each one of you I send my old message—

" Good Luck and - - - CARRY ON."

C. W. Mustill.

Lt.-Col.

Bramley Barracks,
   Leeds,
      15 *December*, 1944.

POST

DOENITZ
ANNOUNCES
THE END

Although the German surrender was expected, the official announcement was not made until 8 May 1945 – Victory in Europe (VE) day. Here people in Leeds queue to buy the **Yorkshire Evening Post** containing details of Germany's final collapse. Schools were closed, workers were given a holiday, and thanksgiving services were held in Leeds churches.

Soldiers and civilians celebrate victory by carrying an effigy of Hitler down Briggate. Flags, paper hats, drink and even a cigar are in evidence (as well as a woman wearing the ubiquitous 'pinnie') but the children look slightly bemused.

There were two camps for German prisoners of war in the Leeds area, no. 244 at Butcher Hill, Horsforth and no. 91 at Post Hill Camp, Farnley. The prisoners at Butcher Hill produced their own magazine **Die Brücke**. In this photograph prisoners from Farnley can be seen roadbuilding. The Germans remained as prisoners until 1947.

Victory party at Hillcrest Avenue, Harehills. Hundreds of
these were held in the city following VE Day, 8 May 1945.

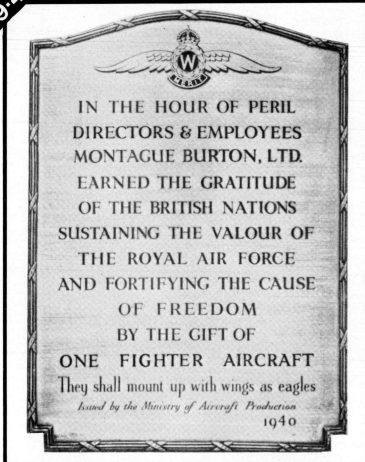

IN THE HOUR OF PERIL
DIRECTORS & EMPLOYEES
MONTAGUE BURTON, LTD.
EARNED THE GRATITUDE
OF THE BRITISH NATIONS
SUSTAINING THE VALOUR OF
THE ROYAL AIR FORCE
AND FORTIFYING THE CAUSE
OF FREEDOM
BY THE GIFT OF
ONE FIGHTER AIRCRAFT
They shall mount up with wings as eagles
Issued by the Ministry of Aircraft Production
1940

As a major clothing manufacturer Montague Burton, along with other Leeds firms, played a vital role in the wartime production of garments and uniforms. The company provided these two floats as part of Leeds' contribution to the London Victory Parade on 8 June 1946. Workers at Burton's also collected money for a Spitfire in 1940. This plaque can be seen in Hudson Road Mills.

Uniforms and Equipment

5,500,000 battle dress blouses.
6,250,000 battle dress trousers.
3,000,000 Army greatcoats (various types).
1,500,000 suits, demobilisation.
75,000 raincoats, demobilisation.
75,000 overcoats, demobilisation.
100,000 suits, denim overalls.
75,000 mackinaws (U.S.A. Forces).
100,000 suits, hospital blue.
1,000,000 R.A.F. jackets and blouses.
250,000 R.A.F. trousers.
75,000 R.A.F. greatcoats.
85,000 windproof suits (smocks and trousers).
90,000 duffle coats.
150,000 C.D., N.F.S., etc., jackets, blouses and trousers.
280,000 C.D., N.F.S., etc., greatcoats, overcoats and raincoats.
50,000 trousers for U.S.A. Forces.
150,000 khaki drill trousers.
700,000 drill shorts (khaki and green).
60,000 anti-mosquito slacks.
50,000 anti-mosquito skirts.
50,000 snow suits.
400,000 miscellaneous outer garments in quantities of less than 50,000 each.
58,000,000 cartridge bags.
46,000,000 exploder bags.
7,500,000 igniter, fuse filling, burster and H.E. bags.
275,000 labels for seamen's exposure suits.
1,450,000 labels for water purifying bags for jungle use.
120,000 labels for anti-mosquito wallets.
1,501,000 flashes of tartan cloth.
600,000 P.O.W. flashes.
115,000 insignia for 5th Infantry Division.
5,000,000 combat insignia for U.S. troops.
5,000 jungle epalettes for nursing sisters.

3,200,000 service strips to denote branch.
120,000 insignia for U.S.A.A.F. flying personnel.
20,000 bandoliers for 50 rounds of rifle ammunition.
168,000 wallets for anti-mosquito protective equipment.
85,624,000 felt sweat strips for anti-gas eyeshields.
Also thousands of million utility labels and millions of size tickets for clothing contracts.
1,250,000 drogues (ammunition component).
250,000 muzzle covers (rubberised).
1,000,000 silica gel. and powder bags.
500,000 packing discs.
5,500,000 yards webbing (various widths).
250,000 yards tracing tapes.
250,000 rifle covers.
4,250,000 cotton bags for rations, messages, etc.
750,000 shirt collars.
500,000 cotton cellular drawers.
9,250,000 arm badges, flashes and patches.
2,250,000 sizing tickets and labels.
3,750,000 pads for sleeves and shoulders of suits.
1,000,000 flags.
1,250,000lbs. flock.
1,700 tons cordage.
350,000 caps (various types).
170,000 overalls and gowns.
165,000 bolster cases.
100,000 mine markers.
100,000 anti-mosquito outfits.
122,000 kerchiefs.
100,000 toe covers (mountain and snow equipment).
110,000 physical training shorts.
75,000 shirts.
50,000 pyjama suits.
50,000 blanket bags.

Munitions

Give us the tools, and we will finish the job.
THE PRIME MINISTER.

Production included :

2,000 carriages for 25 pdr. gun.
400 6 pdr. anti-tank guns.
870 locomotives.
143,000 hand grenades.
1,880,000 anti-tank grenades.
3,000,000 2inch mortar bomb tail units.
175,000 transit plugs for 2inch mortar bombs.
900,000 tail units for 30lb. incendiary bombs.
119,000 jet valve bodies.
350 gun barrels and 2,000 recuperatures for 17 pdr. anti-tank guns.
650 transmissions and 350 sets of suspension units for Valentine tanks.
700 final drive assemblies for Churchill tanks.
4,000 breech rings for 25 pdr. guns and 350 breech mechanisms.
300 carriages for 17 pdr. anti-tank guns and 1,000 breech mechanisms.
400 printing machines.
85,000,000 feet of light alloy tubing for aircraft production.
87,500,000 feet of brass, copper and bronze tubing.
63,000,000 driving bands for shells.
250,000 pairs of binoculars and other optical instruments.
12,000,000 paper and cardboard components for ammunition.
95,000,000 insulated discs for bombs and shells.
33,000 500lb. incendiary transit crates.
3,000,000 igniter and burster bags for exploding shells.
1,298,500 5.5 inch charge bags to hold propellant charges.
1,160,000 25 pdr. charge bags.

8,392,500 exploder bags to explode anti-aircraft shells.
180,000 6-inch charge bags.
142,000 7.2-inch charge bags.
242,000 4.5-inch charge bags.
Also millions of spools for self-adhesive tape for sealing signals; several hundred thousand small parts for Bailey bridges, aircraft, wireless, Naval construction, etc.
5,628 machine tools.
898 locomotives and electric trucks.
406 steam turbines.
156 cordite presses and rolling mills.
3,542 H.F. generator sets.
2,441 electric generators and motors.
900,000,000 .303 inch cartridges.
5,000,000 15 mm. cartridges.
8,500,000 20mm. cartridge cases.
500,000 20 mm. projectiles.
30,000,000 shells.
726 Lancasters.
3,920 Ansons and spares equivalent to nearly 1,000 more Ansons.
1,560 tanks.
120 diesel locomotives.
9 other items :
Soap, Swordfish aircraft components, springs for Army road vehicles and tanks, Halifax bomber electric wiring, assault landing craft, machine tools, units for Mulberry ports, parts for landing strips at sea, rifle barrels, coil springs.

The above list is incomplete as official figures of the engineering production of the City are not available.

Part of the wartime production by industry in Leeds. From **Leeds To Victory**, the **Yorkshire Evening Post's** remarkable catalogue of the output of those who fought on the home front.

On 13 May 1945 over 2000 took part in a victory
parade of auxiliary units through the city centre. Shelters
were closed and plans made to demolish them. Mr F. Gregory,
who had run the **Yorkshire Evening Post's** problem page
throughout the war, faced a barrage of letters about demob
and bleaching blackout curtains.

1939·45

Repatriated prisoners of war look happy to be back in Leeds. In Stalag Luft VI, R.B. Pape, who had worked on the **Yorkshire Post** before joining the RAF, edited the 'Kriegie Edition' of his paper, printing items submitted by members of the White Rose Club.

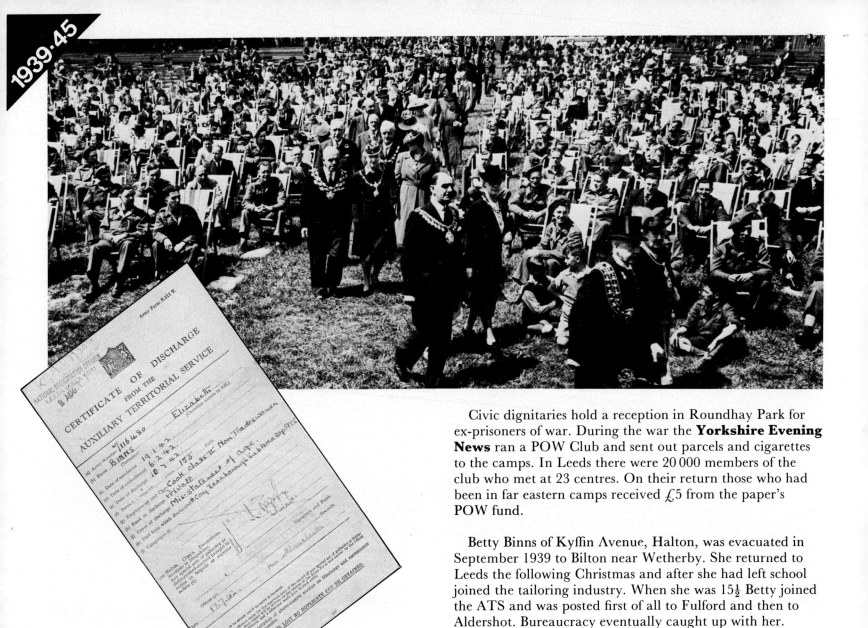

Civic dignitaries hold a reception in Roundhay Park for ex-prisoners of war. During the war the **Yorkshire Evening News** ran a POW Club and sent out parcels and cigarettes to the camps. In Leeds there were 20 000 members of the club who met at 23 centres. On their return those who had been in far eastern camps received £5 from the paper's POW fund.

Betty Binns of Kyffin Avenue, Halton, was evacuated in September 1939 to Bilton near Wetherby. She returned to Leeds the following Christmas and after she had left school joined the tailoring industry. When she was 15½ Betty joined the ATS and was posted first of all to Fulford and then to Aldershot. Bureaucracy eventually caught up with her.

Fred Haigh was fire watching in Bedford Street when the old City Museum was bombed in 1941. At 18 Fred joined the Royal Navy and was posted to **HMS Eskimo** at Scapa Flow. He took part in the Sicily landings and sailed on Arctic and Atlantic convoys. Here the **Eskimo** can be seen racing through convoy PQ 18 being attacked by German bombers. On the return from Russia they ran out of tinned food and vegetables and were on short rations for $5\frac{1}{2}$ days. Back home they were given clothing for Arctic voyages and then sent to the Mediterranean.

Fred returned home and married Betty Binns at Corpus Christi church, Halton, on 1 August 1945. Betty borrowed a dress as did her bridesmaids. Neighbours chipped in with coupons, the beer was brought from the off-licence in a pram, and a reception was held at the Pavilion. The next day Fred went back to sea but later came home to a job on the trams and, eventually, a prefab.

8th June, 1946

TO-DAY, AS WE CELEBRATE VICTORY, I send this personal message to you and all other boys and girls at school. For you have shared in the hardships and dangers of a total war and you have shared no less in the triumph of the Allied Nations.

I know you will always feel proud to belong to a country which was capable of such supreme effort; proud, too, of parents and elder brothers and sisters who by their courage, endurance and enterprise brought victory. May these qualities be yours as you grow up and join in the common effort to establish among the nations of the world unity and peace.

George R.I.

Acknowledgements
The author would like to thank all those who have helped in the preparation of this book, in particular:
T.W.J. Auty; Elaine Bissett; Laurence Chappell; Norman Crowther; Angela Dalby; Michael Dawson; Christina Deri; Olive Denton; Michael and Lesley Farley; George Lane Fox; Brian Gaunt; Jim Gibbons; Fred and Betty Haigh; Malcolm Hulme; the staff of the Imperial War Museum; the Curator, Regimental Museum, Imphal Barracks, York; David Ingham; Brian Jackson; the staff of the Leeds Public Libraries; R.W. Mack and Peter Murton of the RAF Museum, Hendon; Mary and Michael Malone; Caroline and Eddie Maund; C.W. Mustill; David Oxley; Michael and Pat Page; J.B. Parkin of the Leeds Transport Historical Society; Dave Robinson; Michael, Margaret and Betty Scally; Tony Stevens; the staff of the University Library Leeds.

The author is grateful to the following for permission to reproduce photographs:
Montague Burton Ltd.: 92
Co-operative Society, Leeds: 59 (lower right), 75, 84
Daily Mail Newspapers: 63
Hunslet Engine Co. Ltd.: 30 (upper)
Imperial War Museum: Title page, 15, 16, 17, 30 (lower), 43, 44, 45, 78, 97 (top left)
Kirkstall Forge: 14, 79
C.W. Mustill: 57, 64 (left), 68, 71, 72, 86, 87
M.J. O'Connor: 74 (upper right)
R.N. Redman: 81
Roundhay School: 55
Tramway Museum, Crich (R.B. Parr collection): 74 (upper left)
Yorkshire Post Newspapers Ltd.: 24 (lower), 28, 38, 40, 45, 53 (left), 66 (left), 74, 75, 89, 93